Living Flame Series

VOLUME FOURTEEN

Saint Teresa on Prayer

Jerome Lantry O.C.D.

Edited by
THOMAS CURRAN O.C.D.

CARMELITE CENTRE OF SPIRITUALITY

Carmelite Centre of Spirituality
Avila Morehampton Road Dublin 4, Ireland.

ISBN 0 86088 025 7

Cum permissu superiorum

Preface

This book contains much of the basic teaching of St Teresa on prayer and gives a brief summary of her main writings on this topic. But it is not a comprehensive study of her writings. For the most part it limits itself to just one of her books, *The Way of Perfection* (WP). The purpose she had in writing that was to teach some nuns close to her how to make mental prayer. This present writing presents her teaching to anyone interested in prayer. By means of summary, quotation and comment, it puts the *Way of Perfection* within your reach. Since it follows the plan she used, there may be some repetition but this effects a helpful emphasis. A special effort has been made to remain close to her thought and style so that the inspiration of her own words would not be lost.

CONTENTS

Introduction

In our times, so many, many people are turning to prayer in one form or another. This is great news and there are lots of clear indications that it is not just a passing trend but something real. There is a search on today for something spiritual that is genuine and permanent. We have gone through so much change that we are wondering what is permanent, on what can we depend. St Teresa did some careful thinking on all that too and had a few thoughts that she wrote down and kept as a bookmark to keep her thinking straight. It said:

> Let nothing disturb thee;
> Let nothing dismay thee;
> All things pass;
> God never changes.
> Patience attains
> All that it strives for.
> He who has God
> Finds he lacks nothing:
> God alone suffices.

Here we have some of the basic ideas that occur and re-occur in her writing. So that she had clearly decided that nothing is permanent and changeless but God himself. Customs and laws, plans and structures can change, adjust or even disappear when they have served their purposes. New ideas grow old and give way to newer ones. People come and go and even the indispensable ones move on. It takes time and thought to come even to a vague awareness of what St Teresa has written on her bookmark. So the people who find God in their lives find the one permanent thing there is and come to realise little by little that God fulfils all their needs, that God alone can do that. It is this thought or intuition that draws people to pray. At first they crave for some sense of God that can be felt, to which they react in an emotional way, in sorrow or joy or a blending of both. In time they learn to be aware of God in a much quieter and deeper way. It becomes a new world of truth and freedom, of light and love. This is human life in full flower. People who find this way develop a great emotional balance, a deeper insight into life and even a clearer intellect.

One other basic thing in St Teresa's life was her love for the Church. This may not sound that enticing to us if we have grown confused about the Church. If so, we are missing something very important and basic. The Church is not a building, not a highly structured and rich organisation. The Church is the people. The Church came into being at Pentecost. The people chosen by Christ as the first members of the Church, the apostles, were all present but incapable of doing anything until the Holy Spirit came; then they were new people, who preached fearlessly and continued to bring the faith to thousands in spite of being jailed, beaten and even banished. This early group of Christians came to speak of themselves simply as the assembly and the word 'Church' is just a translation of that. This assembly was more than the group of people who were members of it. By a special gift of God, they were given a share in the very life of Christ, so that they were united to him just as parts of a human body share the human life that is in them; just like branches of a tree share the life of the tree. This was brought home dramatically to St Paul at his conversion. When Jesus spoke to him, he said, 'Why do you persecute me?' He did not ask why he was persecuting his followers. He did not make that distinction. So, when we come to Jesus Christ in prayer, we come to all people. When we learn to pray, we are with God our Father and with his Son, who is not just my Redeemer and yours but the Redeemer of all people. Prayer is something we frequently do alone, just as Jesus did, but in prayer we are not turning our back on people. Rather, we reach out to them. Their welfare is our concern because it is God's concern.

St Teresa's awareness of God involved her more and more in the cares of the Church, but we must bear in mind that her notion of the Church was very personal. It was Christ. In the members of the Church she saw Christ praised, served, persecuted, shamed, let down or glorified. Many times she spoke of a great wish to give her life and to give it a thousand times to save one human being from the consequences of sin. And this is exactly what Christ's life and death were all about so that we can in a way see the love of Christ for us reflected in the life of the Saint. If prayer brings us close to God and helps us to grow in our love for him, then his will becomes our will and his will is that people, all people, should come to him. By knowing him and by knowing what he has done

6

and is doing for them, they come to know their own worth and dignity. This is the way to peace and unity, the way to end crime and injustice and war. St Teresa was aware of these things and was not turning aside but coming to help when she spent long hours in silent prayer, alone with God, her God and our God.

St Teresa did not stop to make distinctions between Christ and the Church. Her love of Christ was a really beautiful thing. It comes out in the way she speaks of him. It is so very prayerful and human, sometimes mingling complaints with humour, joy with sacrifice, that you keep on reading to see what she will say next. She talks of him as a friend and companion, a loving teacher, a poor suffering man who must not be left alone, a great victorious king who has conquered a kingdom and wants to give it to you. Many times her instruction or narrative is broken and she is writing prayer, sometimes praising, sometimes pleading but always so close to reality and so close to God. It must have been this awareness of God's majesty and our littleness that gave her such a great sense of humour. It made her realistic about people, holding up to them the highest ideals and yet insisting on good sense and acceptance of limitations. She is certainly a most lovable saint and she seems to be saying so often, so persuasively, 'If it happened to me, I cannot see why it would not happen to you.'

1.   St Teresa's Writings

St Teresa was absolutely certain of the value of prayer in our lives and she went to great lengths to teach and even coax people to pray. She did this not just for her own nuns but for all her friends and that meant for many lay people and priests. This was her favourite gift. One might say her way of saying: 'I love you' was: 'Let me help you to pray'. She was a woman who was gifted with a quick mind and a most attractive personality. She made friends easily and summed up situations quickly. She was not easily satisfied and in her relentless search she found God in prayer. Like the man in the Gospel who found the treasure in the field and who sold all that he had and bought the field, she found God in prayer and gave her life to this special field. It became her apostolate. Through this she supported the Church, sanctified its priests, spread the Gospel to new peoples and lived the fullest Christian life anyone could hope to experience. The story of her great life is told in her writings. In a collection of her writings, you will find long books and short accounts of incidents in her life. You can gather from these a good account of how she spent her years but, first and foremost, those books are about prayer. They tell of prayer itself or of how she established communities dedicated to prayer and the many negotiations this work entailed. Always the theme is prayer, and prayer is the purpose of the relentless effort. And all this because God is found in prayer and God is the only answer, the full answer to the multiple searchings of the human heart. No matter what you read by St Teresa, it will turn your mind to God because she had come to that kind of friendship with God that she was aware of him everywhere, whether she was happy or sad, busy or quiet. But there are a few books in particular to which people go for instruction on prayer. The one that is generally recognised as being her best is the last one she wrote, *The Interior Castle*, (IC) sometimes referred to as *The Mansions*. This book was written in 1577, five years before her death. The whole concept of the book is very close to the biblical teaching that we are the temples of the Holy Spirit. St Teresa speaks of the person at prayer as being a castle in which God lives in a central mansion surrounded by six other mansions, each with its own apartments. The seven mansions represent stages of prayer from that of being in the state of grace or being clear of serious sin (First Mansion) to full mystical union with God (Seventh Mansion). The first, second and third mansions deal with the life of prayer we can develop by our own efforts with the ordinary graces God gives to all of us. The other four have to do with stages of prayer that can come only with special help from God.

The second book that is considered a main source of St Teresa's teaching on prayer is the book of her *Life* (L), sometimes referred to as her autobiography. This book was written in 1556 but that account was lost. So she was told to re-write it and did so in 1565. Chapters I-X of this book tell of her early years insofar as they lead to her dedication to a life of prayer. And then in Chapters XI-XXII she gives us a kind of booklet on prayer and what it is all about. Here she speaks of the praying person as an orchard that is made fruitful by being watered and tells of four different ways in which the water comes. The water, of course, is God's grace and so the four different ways of watering the garden are God's different ways of helping us to pray. The first way is to draw water from a well and this is prayer we can develop by our own efforts so that it would be on the same level as mansions I-III. The second way of watering is to have a water-wheel rigged up with buckets so you can turn the wheel and draw so much more water with little effort. This is the beginning of prayer we cannot come to by our own effort but only with the special help of God. Yet even here we do contribute by being attentive to what he is doing and cooperating with his special graces. The third way of watering is an advance on the second. The water comes along in a stream which we just direct here and there. In prayer this means we have less to do but still must cooperate in a smaller way. The final way of watering is simply by means of heavy rain when the Lord does it all and we just enjoy his goodness.

For those learning to pray, both this section of the *Life* and all of *The Interior Castle* are worth reading. They are immensely helpful and instructive. Both were written in obedience to superiors who wanted her teaching on prayer and we are most grateful to those men who recognised the value of her experience and were responsible for getting so much of it for us in writing. *The Way of Perfec-*

tion (WP), however, was written for some of her own nuns who just wanted to get some help for themselves so that they could grow in prayer. So it is geared to getting people to pray and to instructing them in some practical matters that can help or hinder our progress in communicating with God. At first the book was written like a long personal letter to a small group of nuns living with her. Later, when she saw it would be used in other houses too, she re-wrote it. This second copy is the one that is normally used but modern editions all include passages from the first version so that none of her thought is lost. The plan is simple and easy to pick up from the headings of the chapters. She begins with a short prologue that creates immediate interest because she tells us why she is writing the book — the nuns asked her to do so and because of their love for her the few things she has to say will be taken to heart by them. She also lists her sources — experience gained (a) in her life, (b) in dealing with others, (c) through what God has taught her in prayer. No doubt about it, she is writing from her own experience. When St Teresa began to experience God's presence in very deep ways in prayer, she wisely went to a confessor for advice. Many failed to understand her and she did not meet many who had similar experiences themselves. One of them asked her to write an account of what happened when she prayed. This was really the beginning of her writing. She was so clear in her description of delicate personal experience that she was told to write many times. This description of things that would escape the attention of many is very interesting and makes for a personal style of writing that is full of real life. Chapters I-III of *The Way of Perfection* say why she founded a community given to prayer: to help the Church. Chapters IV-XV deal with three Gospel virtues essential to a life of prayer: love of one another, detachment from created things and true humility. Chapters XVI-XXVI deal mainly with contemplation, its ideals and demands. Chapters XXVII-XLII are a personal commentary on the Our Father and form a special work on prayer from recollection to prayer of union. So the plan of the book is simple and the style is personal and it is no exaggeration to say that this little book coaxes you to pray.

2. A Strong Resolution

Much has been said and written on prayer and yet not many people seem to succeed in making prayer a way of life. The difficulty lies, to some extent, in the lack of resolution. This point is so important, so vital, that there is no way to highlight it too much. It is a known fact that St Teresa had a great problem in getting herself down to the daily practice of prayer and we can see the struggle she had from her own words: 'Very often, over a period of several years, I was more occupied in wishing my hour of prayer were over, and in listening whenever the clock struck, than in thinking of things that were good. Again and again, I would rather have done any severe penance that might have been given me than practise recollection as a preliminary to prayer. . . afterwards, when I had forced myself to pray, I would find that I had more tranquillity and happiness than at certain other times when I had prayed because I had wanted to' (L, 8).

St Teresa is not alone in this teaching. Fulton Sheen made a Holy Hour every day and readily confessed that this was the fountain of faith from which he drew anything he had to offer. Fr James Borst tells how, after years of evasion, he got down to spending an hour a day in prayer, and that it felt so long he thought it was just stubbornness kept him there.

This does not sound encouraging. It is not easy to grow in prayer and yet we must begin and somehow we must succeed. Not to get down to the habit of praying is the biggest mistake one can make. We put it off and find alternative activities; we read, work, discuss, even pray in groups, go to lots of Masses and so on. All of these things are good but can be a hundred times better if we get down to silent, solitary prayer, alone with God. This is frightening, or at least something inside us says so, and we shun it. If you are an average, good Christian, you have been shunning this for years. Frankly, you need help and one sure place to find it is a little book St Teresa wrote for a small group of her friends, *The Way of Perfection*.

Time and again she appeals to us to make up our minds once for all that, come what may, we are going to give time to quiet prayer, and no matter how dull, flat, dry-as-dust it becomes, we will go on and on. She calls not just for a resolution but for one that is strong, not just honest determination but the kind that is really determined. Do not think this is too much for you because she will encourage, exhort, challenge, plead with and support you at every turn. This is what St Teresa does. She does not just instruct you in how to pray. She takes you by the hand and leads you to God and lets you stand before him, humble, grateful, glad to be there, reverent, afraid to offend but not afraid to receive and return love. To love God! Can you? Do you dare? Is this your thing? Let her tell you.

God Loves Us

In the book of her *Life,* she says this: 'Mental prayer, it seems to me, is nothing else than to communicate in friendship many times alone, with him who we know loves us' (L, 8). From this description and from the whole paragraph, there is evidence of a personal friendship built around the fact that God loves us and is waiting for us to respond. If you examine this carefully and find that this is the way you think, you are very lucky. So many people think of themselves as being unlovable in God's eyes that they are not at all ready to come near him in prayer. When St Peter first got an inkling of who Jesus was, he told him to go away and the reason he gave is still being used: 'I am a sinful man.' To be in sin and to tell the Saviour to go away and not tell him to come and cure us is foolish and yet it is what we are doing every day. This 'depart-from-me-Lord' way of thinking had become so much a habit with us we do not realise how often it triggers our reflexes and turns us away from anything that might have brought us face to face with God, our Father, our Creator, our Redeemer, our Friend.

St Teresa's idea of God as the one who knows all things, who can do all things and who loves me is worth thinking over at some length. It is good to hear but we can too easily walk away and forget it. To learn what God is like we search the Bible and there we see God first as the Creator of things. He is the beginning, never created, never having to learn or to grow in any way because he is perfect in every possible way. It is an easy conclusion from this that God is infinitely good. Goodness wants to give and all creation is the result of God wanting to share his happiness. The living God who slumbers not nor sleeps, is vigilant, benevolent and all-powerful. The Bible tells how he made a covenant with human beings like us. It was not usual for one to make a pact of that kind with someone inferior to him and for God to make such an agreement with the people he had created was a real revelation of his goodwill. As the people became aware of what God had done, we find the Bible expressing the story of the covenant in song with all the language of high romance: the King falling in love with the pauper. He is not put off by our unworthiness. This is what the incarnation is all about. The song of the angels at Bethlehem gives the message: peace on earth to men who are the object of God's goodwill. Every book in the Bible should be read in this light. For now let us look at the fifteenth chapter of St Luke's Gospel. In that narrative, Jesus was criticised for being a friend of publicans and sinners and for eating with them. He replied by telling three parables illustrating the mercy of God. We are familiar with the story of the lost sheep, the lost coin and the prodigal son. We have often thought about them, comparing ourselves with the sheep, the coin or the sinner. It is well to reflect that we also get three pictures of what God is like. He is like the shepherd who searches through wide open spaces for you, for me. Why? Because we are his and we have strayed from him. He does not sit and wait to see if we will come back but he leaves everything and comes to look for us. God is like a woman who loses a coin. She has nine more and is not in need but the lost one is hers and she goes to look for it. This search is slow and careful but yet persevering and successful. The coin cannot come home of itself and yet is returned to its rightful place. And God, our Father, is like the father of the prodigal son. He waited and waited for the wayward one to come and was filled with pity as soon as he saw him. That is a rare picture of God, an old man running out of love for his sinner son who was lost and is found. These are not parables to be put aside but to be put inside in the heart and pondered on frequently. We sinners are not servants but friends.

God is like that; he hates sin but loves the sinner even while he is in sin. God does not wait for us to be good before he loves us. God loves us before we do a thing, long before we merit anything, when we have nothing to offer. Our minds are like sick people trying to get back to health. They need good warm days and fresh air and they need to sit or walk around enjoying this lovely weather. So too with God's love. We have to wait in it to be made healthy by it,

13

to let it tan our entire attitude to things. It is the greatest of all mistakes to say to God, 'Depart from me.' You must correct that and say to him, 'Come to me, I will wait for you, find time alone for you. I will trust my whole future to your love for me.'

God created you, made you out of nothing. You were not and now you are. Isn't this an enormous commitment? God made you and he will make something great out of you no matter how you feel about yourself. Your sinfulness will not stop him. St John tells us this: 'God loved the word so much that he gave his only Son, so that everyone who believes in him may not be lost but may have eternal life' (Jn 3:16). He also says: 'This is the love I mean, not our love for God but God's love for us when he sent his Son to be the sacrifice that takes our sins away' (4:10). If God loves you enough to make you out of nothing, and to send to Calvary his beloved Son in whom he was so well pleased, then our tendency to shy away from God is wrong and lacking in faith and confidence. It takes time and work to reverse this trend, and yet, such a change is necessary. It helps a whole lot to talk to those who are aware of God's love, to read whatever brings it home to us and, in particular, to search the scriptures with the set purpose of learning this lesson from the Holy Spirit. St Teresa says prayer is having to do with him who we know loves us. If we know this, we will find it easier to spend time alone with him and to do that often.

3.   As We Live We Pray

Another basic point in St Teresa's teaching is that life and prayer go hand in hand. This is very important and has some implications worth noting. We know from the scriptures and all the teaching of the saints that, unless we are doing our best to carry out God's will, to live by our conscience, we are not giving God a chance to do all he has planned for us. What is especially interesting in St Teresa is the source of her information. In the very beginning of *The Way of Perfection* she says: 'I shall speak of nothing of which I have no experience, either in my own life or in the observation of others, or which the Lord has not taught me in prayer' (WP, Prologue).

It is worth noting here that St Teresa says that the desire to

14

change our ways comes from prayer and that even if we fail to change, we should keep on praying and not give up, because we will ultimately change our ways. She also makes the very noteworthy point that, if we hope to advance to real contemplation, we have to develop in our actual way of living three habits or virtues: love of our neighbour, self-denial and humility. At no time does she quote the Gospel as the source for this teaching so that it may well have come from her own experience and yet, the three things she singles out as essential to contemplatives are the very same three things that Christ emphasised as being in some way personal to himself. Of love of neighbour he said it was a new commandment, his commandment, the quality by which all would recognise us as his disciples. Of self-denial, he said it was essential to following him, which is synonymous with living the Gospel. We must deny ourselves, take up our cross and be his disciples, his close followers. Of humility, he said, 'Learn of me for I am meek and humble of heart.' It is essential that we note how personal to Christ these virtues are, as if he were saying that he insisted on them in his close friends. Nor is it a mere coincidence that we find the following in the document on the Church in Vatican II. We read: 'The Church, consequently, equipped with the gifts of her Founder, and faithfully guarding his precepts of charity, humility and self-denial, receives the mission to proclaim and establish among all peoples the Kingdom of Christ and of God' (*Lumen Gentium*, 6). And it would seem that Christ taught these to St Teresa. Is it too much to suppose that he is more than willing and able to teach them to us?

In teaching these three virtues to her nuns, St Teresa takes lots of examples from day-to-day convent life, examples that would not always apply in other circumstances but one who wants to grow in prayer and asks Christ for help with these essential qualities of living will meet practical examples every day. Take love of neighbour. St Paul, in trying to emphasise the fact that love of neighbour is the greatest charism of all, says: 'Love is always patient and kind; it is never jealous; love is never boastful or conceited; it is never rude or selfish; it does not take offence, and is not resentful. Love takes no pleasure in other people's sins but delights in the truth; it is always ready to excuse, to trust, to hope, and to endure whatever comes' (1 Cor 13:4-7).

15

All of the sixteen chapters of 1 Corinthians are worth careful study in the matter of prayer to see what is permanent and what is not. But, in particular, we can take a few points from the passage quoted and start to work on them day by day. Divide it into some *DO'S* and *DON'TS*. Don't be selfish, boastful, resentful. Do be kind, patient, forgiving, persevering. Try it and the concrete situations will emerge. Out of this experiment you will begin to see in yourself some real failures in Christian living. Do not run away from them. The very fact that you can face them will make you a forgiving, tolerant person, slow to condemn and a good patient listener. This is a real solid beginning on which to build.

Real down-to-earth love will call for generosity. It really comes to life when it makes demands. This is the double line between using someone to love ourselves and really loving people for their own sake. St Teresa is very insistent on unselfish ways if we are to develop a life of prayer. In this matter, as with charity and humility, she directs us repeatedly to compare ourselves with Christ and learn from him. This makes sense. If we accept the fact that he lived his life and died and rose for us, then we try to live for him and to be just a little like him in the way we live. It is so easy to accept all this as a teaching and never put it into practice; which is just saying it is right but it is really up to someone else to act on it. No, you must go with St Teresa to look at Christ in his passion and to bring home to yourself that this special friend went through all this for you. A young mother carrying one child and trying to save two more from being run down by cars said to her own mother: 'I never realised you went through this with us.' This is the kind of 'realising' we need to do with Christ in the Gospels. This is what will bring out a response in our own lives and the only way you can love God is by realising his love for you and responding to it. This is what St Teresa called the standard coin for loving God. Not the high moment of mystic experience but the doing or enduring unselfishly to thank him for his splendid, unlimited sacrifice in which he loved you more than his own comfort.

St Teresa reminds us of the good things God has done for us and calls on us to praise and thank him. There is great wisdom in this. We really need to count our blessings to find the hidden benefits in our trials, to list them clearly and thank him for them one by one. From here we can move into the fruitful field of things offered to

God and learn to let the grain of wheat die on the way to harvest. In this too we can learn from St Teresa, who advises us to make use of the trials already in our lives before we even think of doing anything beyond that.

There are many things we have to go without because we cannot afford them. This 'state of being without' is really a place where God is waiting for you. Compare your life with that of Christ. Did he have the thing you regret being unable to afford? Can you find consolation in the fact that you share this lack with him? Does it delight you? He loves a cheerful giver. From here you will come to give to the poor for his sake. If Christ is our treasure and our heart is given to him, then the old human urge to make the million makes no sense, unless we gather it for his needy ones. But material things are not the only things that get between us and God. We get far too concerned about our health and comfort. St Teresa told her nuns to be 'manly' about such things and not to be preoccupied about small illnesses and unnecessary comforts. It is against a very personal matter that differs from one to another and from place to place. But look into the things you do every day and see, are you over-concerned about health and ruining it through lack of discipline? Here again is an area of self-denial, a place to compare yourself with Christ, to deny yourself in ways that will let him live in you. Today we are more aware of our psychological make-up. Here again we find much to work on, things to change and things to live with, moods in need of attention and change, reactions and sensitivities that will not change unless we can talk to God about them. St Teresa is very strong on 'self-knowledge' and in her language this means something highly practical: we note objectively how we act or fail to act, ask ourselves why and try little by little with God's help to change.

In the scriptures, we see the Holy Spirit as one who removes 'impossible' barriers. It is a real sign of God-in-us to see some of our self-built walls crumbling and new freedom coming to flower. Without him we can do nothing but in him we can do all things. The final point in all this area is the surrender of our will to God's will. Teresa takes this up in many places and gives it a lengthy treatment in different books. She looks carefully at what Christ himself did and how he accepted the Father's will, even when he knew that meant death. Then she says that when he taught us to say, 'Thy will be done', he was asking us to join with him in this giving of our will to the Father. Also, she reminds us that we are no heroes in this but are just making a virtue of accepting and willing what is bound to happen anyway.

Resignation is not enough; we must give our will gladly and see that real action follows our promise. Not an easy matter but a very fruitful exercise: 'What power this gift has! If it be made with due resolution, it cannot fail to draw the Almighty to become one with our lowliness and to transform us into himself and to effect a union between the Creator and the creature' (WP, 22).

Doing God's will is a truly great and Christian work and the sure test of all prayer. This is what is referred to so often in the test, 'By their fruits you shall know them'. But doing God's will is not all that simple. To expect God's will to be spelled out at every turn can lead to scrupulosity. If you are keeping God's commandments, then what you are doing all day is good and pleasing to God. Just as we said about praying to him who we know loves us, also we live our lives each day under the eyes of him who loves us and who is pleased with all we do, so long as it is not sinful. This should help us to enjoy doing his will even when it involves things not pleasant for us. This is the real secret of the saints; to enjoy doing things that are hard for us in order to please him. Through these, we learn the real wisdom that comes from being close to God. There is no place we can get close to Christ so quickly as in his sufferings.

Obviously, this brings us face to face with our own weaknesses. We can see the truth about ourselves and yet not be discouraged by it. And this is what humility is about. It is facing the truth while making sure the mood is right. To be able to come before God with all the respect due to him who made and redeemed us and yet to trust in his goodness, this is the all important basic lesson that makes growth in prayer possible.

Humility is a little subtle. We can think we are humble and yet be secretly proud. There are some indications of real humility. Gratitude is one. To be aware of the goodness of God when things are going badly for us, that is humility. To see any good we find in ourselves as a gift of God; to want to be like Christ when he was accused and remained silent, that is his work within us. Teresa says, 'It takes great humility to find oneself unjustly condemned and be silent, and to do this is to imitate the Lord who set us free

18

from all our sins. I beg you, then to study earnestly to do so, for it brings great gain; whereas, I can see no gain in our trying to free ourselves from blame — none whatever—save, as I say, in a few cases where hiding the truth might cause offence or scandal' (WP, 15).

It was only a great awareness of herself in the presence of God that could make her say: 'We can never be blamed unjustly since we are always full of faults' (WP, 15). Love of neighbour, self-denial and humility were so bound together in St Teresa's thinking that they are inseparable. 'I cannot understand how humility exists, or can exist, without love or love without humility, and it is impossible for these two virtues to exist save where there is great detachment from all created things' (WP, 16).

All through her discussion of these virtues, there is a clear orientation towards the practical. They are not things to write about and explain but something to do, like doing one's work. It is something planned and put into effect. 'We must all try to be preachers by our deeds' (WP, 15). This is the key to the way her mind works. She exhorts, coaxes and encourages and yet does not demand a standard or even a measurable progress. No, she wants practical down-to-earth effort with a great honesty about ourselves. She will glady accept our statement that we are 'no saints' but is very opposed to using this as a reason for not trying. As we live, we pray and, as we pray, we should try to live. It is not enough to give our attention to prayer, we must be always trying to give our life to God. The great basic laws which call us to love God and to love our neighbour apply to prayer as well as to plain living. We cannot learn to pray just by getting hold of some techniques and putting them into practice. This may bring us calm and quiet and leave us with a clear creative mind but, if it is not building a relationship with God who loves us, it is not prayer. If we can, time and again, pick ourselves up out of the dirt of our failures and keep on trying to make ourselves an everlasting gift to him, we have something to bring to prayer. Otherwise, there may be some interesting experiences but they, of themselves, cannot kindle the fire of love and prayer is an exercise in loving even in the darkness of faith and the absences of hope. So, the surest way to build a life of prayer is to take up the instructions of him who teaches us to pray and see how we do in putting them into practice:

19

> I give you a new commandment: love one another; just as I have loved you, you also must love one another. By this love you have for one another, everyone will know that you are my disciples. (Jn 13:34-35)
>
> If anyone wants to be a follower of mine, let him renounce himself and take up his cross and follow me. For anyone who wants to save his life will lose it; but anyone who loses his life for my sake, and for the sake of the Gospel, will save it. (Mk 8:34-35)
>
> Come to me, all you who labour and are overburdened, and I will give you rest. Shoulder my yoke and learn from me, for I am gentle and humble in heart, and you will find rest for your souls. Yes, my yoke is easy and my burden light. (Mt 11:28-30)

Examine these words slowly and carefully. You will see they are the words of a real friend — one who put his life into what he said. Try to respond to these words. Without pretence, fully aware of your failures, begin to do what you can. He will give you courage and strength. You are taking the sure way to prayer.

4. Learning to Pray

While we try to respond to Christ's call to love one another, and to give of ourselves and be humble, we also give time to prayer. We have to discuss them separately but in real life they form part of the same daily living. *We need to learn to pray.* We begin like the apostles by asking Christ to teach us to pray. It is the God who loves us who also teaches us to pray. St Teresa sets about guiding us in prayer in a very simple way. She tells us to begin where we are. We all have been praying for years. We may say we were just reciting prayers but the fact is that we would not have gone on and on with them if they did not do something for us and the something they do is to let us in some degree communicate with God. Teresa says to us to add some more awareness of what we are doing and we are on a sure road to a real life of prayer. Beyond that she does not have a lot to say by way of technique. This new awareness she tries to bring into our prayer by telling us to ask ourselves three questions before we recite the vocal prayer: to whom am I going to speak, who am I, and what am I going to say? Time and again in

The Way of Perfection, she comes back to these three points. It is well worth your while to go to the scriptures and look at people who spoke to God and see the great awareness they had. In the Old Testament, there was Moses who was told to put off his shoes because the ground on which he stood was made holy by the presence of God. There was Samuel who said, 'Speak, Lord, your servant is listening.' In the New Testament, the relationship of Jesus with his Father is something to be studied and pondered. It is the most beautiful thing the world has ever seen. He was very much aware of his own humble state as man and so always spoke with great reverence and yet with total love. The way in which he said, 'Father, my Father, just Father', shows a bond of great, great love and it is into this bond he wants to draw you when he tells you to say, 'Our Father'. But we also have in the New Testament so many cases of people becoming aware of Christ, of the great unknown magnetic something in him. We see it first in Mary, who ponders it all in her heart, who shares his pain and is humbly grateful to be part of it. There are others: the centurion, Jairus, the man whose boy was a lunatic, the blind who saw, the deaf who heard, the cripples and even the dead who walked again, Mary Magdalene at the tomb, the apostles in the upper room, Paul on the way to Damascus. These people knew how to pray — knew that when they turned to pray they were face to face with someone.

God is your Creator. Maybe you know a little of the history of a hundred years ago. People were busy with work, with special problems, with much of what concerns us. Yet none of us was there. We simply were not. Now we are. We are here—before God. He made us. He made us out of nothing. So we stand before him in great humility, remembering our origins, conscious of our roots. And yet grateful. He saw us as possible persons and made us actual human beings. He who is mighty has surely done a great thing for me in bringing me into existence. The first response in all honesty must be adoration, but love goes with it. He made us because of his goodness. It was a work of love, and love is the response that expresses our gratitude. When we see ourselves and see how little we are and how frequently we have failed, we soon ask for forgiveness. This is the way, too, that Teresa asks us to proceed. To see ourselves as we are, to examine our conscience and to ask his forgiveness. And she somehow makes it all sound like

21

human politeness: 'When people tell you that they are speaking with God by reciting the *Pater Noster* (Our Father) and thinking of worldly things — well, words fail me. When you speak, as it is right for you to do with so great a Lord, it is well that you should think of who it is that you are addressing, and what you yourself are, if only that you may speak to him with proper respect' (WP, 22). Later, in the same context, she says: 'If you give all due attention to the consideration of these two points before you begin the vocal prayers you are about to say, you will be engaging in mental prayer for a very long time!' (WP, 22). She is asking here for 'due attention' to what we are doing when we say even the simplest prayers. Obviously, this starting point in prayer is very important. It is the moment when psychologically we come face to face with God. It is a time to slow down, to begin to do what the psalm says: 'Be still and know that I am God'. This is a real moment of truth — truth that is at first frightening and then immensely reassuring. To come before him who made us is a mighty lesson in detachment from created things. It is, in this situation, incredible that we would prefer something created to him who created it. It seems so utterly foolish to turn our backs on him thinking we can get more joy, more real happiness from what he has made than we could from himself.

What a senseless thing to be proud in the face of the fact that we came from nothing and are depending on God every second of our existence. How absurd to offend God when we are depending on him for the very energy to do so. This way of thinking is real meditation. Indeed, all meditation should lead us back to the point where we stand face to face with God and know who he is and who we are. It is vital that we learn who God is and who we are at the same time. Trying to learn who we are without coming face to face with God is full of pitfalls but, in his presence, we learn by a kind of deep intuition that we are because of him, that we belong to him, that he is committed to us and takes his delight in us. With this we become aware of our deep unworthiness. The guilt of our wrongdoing can be faced in this hallowed place. We know he knows it all and that is something of a relief. We hide this side of self from others and we strive to hide it from ourselves. But, if we stay still and hang on to this awareness of being face to face with him, we begin in time to become clearly aware of what we already knew in an obscure way, that everything within us is open to him. He sees, he knows and we can say with real truth, I confess. We are aware not only of the trespasses remembered but of a deeper unworthiness rooted in our inner being. And yet, he is right there in love and mercy telling us to come to him. In order to bridge the great divide, he has become like me and has done what I could not do alone, he has made up for all my failures, paid my debts, bought me out of slavery, called me friend and child and called me home. This is God. It is to him I am going to talk when I pray. While we begin with a shivering awareness of ourselves, who we are, what we have done, we move on from there as we grow in confidence. The mercy of God is so beautiful, it lets us look at ourselves just as we are and still feel that everything is not lost, that there is a new beginning for us. We do not have to run away from ourselves. We are accepted as we are and given room and opportunity to grow in his image in which we were first made. This is renewal, making all things new in us.

5.   You Before God

To come face to face with God in our own mind, that is the beginning of mental prayer. Bear in mind always that God loves you. From here there are many ways to proceed. In *The Way of Perfection,* St Teresa picks just one way and follows this through. She works on the principle that, if we say our vocal prayers right, we are making mental prayer — so she tells us to say the best of all prayers, the Our Father, and do it slowly with some awareness of God to whom we are speaking. To take one method like this and stay with it, until you have made a habit of it, is a very necessary thing. When you read a lot about prayer, about schools and methods of prayer and about Eastern ways of deeper awareness, you can fall into the trap of hopping from one method to another. This is fatal because it prevents you from acquiring the perseverance that is so necessary in prayer. Prayer is a part of our life and has its bright days and dull periods for many reasons. No one has ever achieved anything in any field without a lot of patience and real slogging. Many people have given up just when success was within reach and so a great effort ended in failure. All our good resolutions about perseverance in prayer can be undermined by skipping from one method to another. Those who stay with prayer finally come to a 'way' that is their own personal method; but, in the beginning, it is vitally important to select one method and stay with it. This need not be St Teresa's method. Her virtue is not in criticising other methods but in following one and showing how it develops. So she takes vocal prayer. In this there is much to draw on. Now that we are familiar with the prayers in the Missal and with the psalms, these provide excellent material. She took the Our Father and this is familiar to all Christians. This prayer was first given to us as a result of a request made by the apostles: 'Lord, teach us to pray'. So it is really Christ teaching us to pray and we let him do this by keeping our attention on him when we say it. So, the first thing Teresa tells us is 'to think of him often when we repeat it, although our own weakness may prevent us from doing so every time' (WP, 24).

The next direction is to be *alone* when we pray like this, something Christ taught us by example because he frequently went off alone to pray. This is no reflection on prayer in groups but just saying that a life of inner prayer requires that, at set times, we do it alone. This requires some planning. We need to find the time and place. It is most helpful, if possible, to have a set time, place and posture for quiet prayer. This simple routine helps to clear the mind and let our awareness of God come to life. Here again, changing place, time or posture may give a brief 'lift' to our prayer for a while but the patient perseverance with the one way of praying does more to deepen the awareness. Teresa says, 'It is impossible to speak to God and to the world at the same time' (WP, 24). So we must do all we can to keep our full attention for him in prayer. There are times too, when, for reasons we cannot understand, 'God allows his servants for days on end to go through great storms' (WP, 24).

Even when things are calm, we do not many times experience his presence but rather his absence. At these times, she encourages us to persevere. 'Do no suppose that, because we cannot hear him, he is silent. He speaks clearly to the heart when we beg him from our hearts to do so. It would be a good idea for us to imagine that he has taught this prayer to each one of us individually, and that he is continually expounding it to us' (WP, 24). This point deserves a good deal of attention. If we come in quiet awareness to recite this prayer with attention to what we are saying, (perhaps even whispering the words so that we can hear them) and we are also in a general way aware of God lovingly present with us, we come to sense that we are not saying it alone. When we pray we are the heart of the Church and we breath the very life of the Church. When we say the prayer Jesus taught us it comes to us in some small way that 'the Spirit himself and our spirit bear united witness that we are the children of God' (Rom 8:16). You do not pray to the Father alone. Jesus prays with you, or rather, you with him. The Spirit prays in you. You lend your breath to the Church when you pray. In one way or another, try to bend your heart's attention to the fact that God not only calls and invites you to pray, but that Christ prays with you and in you.

It often takes an act of sheer faith to bring this home to you but it is still good to know that your prayer does not depend on your poor efforts. Nor is it impoverished by your wayward moods. To encourage us in this, St Teresa says: 'The Master is never so far away that the disciple needs to raise his voice in order to be heard: he is always right at his side. I want you to understand that, if you are to recite the *Pater Noster* well, one thing is needful, you must not leave the side of the Master who has taught it you' (WP, 24). At other times, she talks also of our Lord being *at our side*. This way of thinking of God being present is not new. It is found in other writings and most notably in the Bible: 'The Lord is your guard and your shade; at your right hand he stands' (Ps 120). It is quite possible that St Teresa found it here or in some other book but she certainly made it her own and comes back to it at different times. It gives a setting for our communication with God. When she recaps her teaching up to this point, she emphasises this presence and makes it quite personal and very human: 'the first thing must be examination of conscience, confession of sin and the signing of yourself with the cross. . . as you are alone you must look for a companion — and who could be a better companion than the very Master who taught you the prayer that you are about to say? Imagine that this Lord himself is at your side and see how lovingly and how humbly he is teaching you — and, believe me, you should stay with so good a friend for as long as you can before you leave him. If you become accustomed to having him at your side, and if he sees that you love him to be there and are always trying to please him, you will never be able, as we put it, to send him away, nor will he ever fail you. He will help you in all your trials and you will have him everywhere. Do you think it is a small thing to have such a friend as that beside you?' (WP, 26) That passage is worth reading time and again. The impression of Christ that comes through from it is surely one that makes you want to know him as a *companion* and a *friend*. She many times pleads with us to make this awareness of him a habit — and tells us to stay with it until it becomes for us a habit we would not think of breaking. She tells us to ask him to be with us and if we go a whole year without acquiring the habit to go on and on trying, and not grudge the time because there is no better way we could spend it. In telling us to go on trying to form this habit of being beside him, she says it is not necessary to have great thoughts or deep insights. 'I am only asking you to look at him. For who can prevent you from turning the eyes of your soul (just for a moment if you can do no more) upon this Lord?' (WP, 26) To urge us on again, she says we can surely look at 'the most beautiful thing imaginable' and reminds us that he never takes his eyes off us even when, because of our sins, we are not that pleasant to look at. So, surely, it is no big thing for us to turn away our attention sometimes, at least from other attractions and look at him. It is really a matter of making up our minds to do this: 'If you want him, you will find him' is the way Teresa says it. Just try and he will help you. 'He longs so much for us to look at him once more that it will not be for lack of effort on his part if we fail to do so' (WP, 26).

To give a further push to our effort we are given the example of how a wife tries to please her husband and adapt herself to his moods. We do not have to do this with God. He is the one who adapts himself to our moods. This is an excellent human way of getting across the very important principle that we do not put on appearances before God; we do not try to be someone else or even to change our moods. We start where we are and he comes to us there and where he leads us is his business. Fr John Henaghan said it so well: 'Every man has his secret trail to God. Any soul, at any time, in any place can enter into communion with its Maker. There is no influence nor permission necessary to gain admission to the

Presence. No matter how estranged the outcast, every man can leave the barren country at a moment's notice and come to his Father' (*Pathways to God*, Living Flame, 13, p. 7). We can indeed turn to God in any place at any time. But to do so requires real faith and so very, very often we fail to make this effort of faith that could do us so much good. It is the little pressure that finds the secret door to the hidden treasure we have passed by for so long. The hardest part of praying is to begin. We find it hard in other ways but people who have acquired the habit of giving time regularly to prayer would find it harder to give up than to continue. So whatever the mood, let us not put off the practice of turning our attention to God and letting the eyes of the mind rest on him. St Teresa gives us an example of how to pray when happy or when sad: 'If you are happy, look upon your risen Lord and the very thought of how he rose from the sepulchre will gladden you. How bright and beautiful was he then! How majestic! How victorious! How joyful! He was like one emerging from the battle in which he had gained a great kingdom, which he desired you to have — and with it himself. Is it such a great thing that you should turn your eyes but once and look upon him who made you such great gifts?' (WP, 26). That passage is worth re-reading so as to become more and more aware of what God is like. At great pain he has won for you all you need and he is delighted. Are you? And if you are sad, St Teresa has this to say: 'Look upon him on his way to the Garden. What sore distress he must have borne in his soul, to describe his own suffering as he did and to complain of it. Or look upon him bound to the column, full of pain, his flesh all torn to pieces by his great love for you. How much he suffered, persecuted by some, spit upon by others, denied by his friends, and even deserted by them, with none to take his part, frozen with the cold and left so completely alone that you may well comfort each other' (WP, 26). And she goes on to say he will forget his pain in comforting you because you have come to accompany and comfort him. This blending of your suffering with Christ's passion is the very best thing you can learn in prayer. This is what Christianity is about, to come to the point where, like the apostles, we can rejoice to have been found worthy to suffer something for him.

It sounds like a high ideal, very far away from where we are, but there simply is no Christian alternative and even the weakest beginning will grow in strength. So it is very wise when you experience trials to take them to him in his sufferings and, if you can do nothing else, tell him how much you are hurting. Walk the road to Calvary with him. Take that passage from St Teresa or any meditation like it and start to turn it into your own words until you are saying *your* thoughts, making *your* meditations, having *your* conversation with Christ and *your* pain is joined to his and you feel his love for you in his sacrifices for you and you begin to respond and to see that you are not suffering because of your sins or because God does not care but because he does care and wants to pull you up into life with himself on a closer level. His resurrection and our eternal happiness are the final story and we must always rejoice in the hope it gives, but the here and now is a time of trial in which we need to know the lessons of the passion. Look for a saint who did not lean on the passion for strength and you look in vain. You do need your own meditation on the passion. Every life is a fresh insight into the life of Christ and each new trial tells us new things about his death and resurrection. In time, your meditation will be refined into a simple thought and expressed in a short prayer. But, in the beginning and occasionally later, it is good to express it in detail. Through this prayer you learn to stumble and fall with him and not alone, to love the cross and see it as a blessing. This is a real transformation. If you still need to be convinced that the cross is the sure way to deep prayer, then read Mary Craig's *Blessings*. In it you will meet many people who found new depths to living through the heavy trials life gave them. And St Teresa asks you to look at Mary Magdalene and Mary, the Mother of Jesus, and see how they stood with him in his passion and learn from them that this is the way to go. She tells us to practice enduring small trials, to get a picture of Christ and talk to him about them until it is a habit. She insists you can do this. Technique is *not* the big thing; the will to pray, to get close to him often, until it is a habit, until it is your life — that is the real thing. She also suggests using a book that helps you to pray. She did that for years. Try every way you can to stay at his side. To grow accustomed to this, to make it a solid habit is what makes a real, unbelievable difference in life. This is the place of opportunity, where gold is found, when life begins at any age and goes on eternally. All people live very much by habits they have formed, habits of doing and of not doing. If you are like so many others, you have a habit of not coming close to God, of not being caught alone with him. It is time to change that and make his friendship and companionship a way of life, of new life.

6. Our Father

To pray is to come face-to-face with God in all honesty and humility, yet in confidence as one coming home to his parents. From this position it is easier to call God 'our Father'. This is the very beginning of prayer as Jesus taught it and St Teresa has her own comment. Many excellent things have been written on the subject of God, our Father, beginning with the Bible and going on still. The theology here is deep and will never be complete. St Teresa's comments are not those of a theologian or a scholar. They come from her own living experience and this is a very helpful guide to us in developing our personal relationship with God, our Father. Those who, like St Thérèse of Lisieux, had a special relationship with their own father are off to a good start, but even those who were not so fortunate can find here immense compensation developing unused resources in themselves. History shows that God has revealed his fatherhood in the lives of all sorts of people. He can do all things. What we think we are or have been is no obstacle to him. So you look at what St Teresa has to say with a readiness to believe that while that is personal to her there is something in you that is ready to respond too to God, your Father, if you give yourself the time and opportunity. Prayer begins when we come to ask who is God and the first word in the answer is Father. The word is a revelation of what God is like and how he feels about us. It certainly is an invitation to come to him and to stop acting like a stranger. It is an invitation into heaven itself. And that is Teresa's first reaction. She also sees how much it tells about Christ who, as Son of God, is now made a brother to us and comes to live with us no matter what our state. The very thought of this turns her from her ordinary style of writing into a prayerful address to Christ in which she goes on marvelling at what he has done: giving us everything at once, joining in the prayer of us sinners, and so

29

obliging his Father to accept us as his children, to pardon our sins, to comfort us in trials, to sustain us as fathers do, and more than they can; and finally to share with us the right to inherit all his possessions. This is a beautiful passage that brings to mind some words from St Matthew: 'I bless you, Father, Lord of heaven and of earth, for hiding these things from the learned and the clever and revealing them to mere children. Yes, Father, for that is what it pleased you to do. Everything has been entrusted to me by my Father; and no one knows the Son except the Father, just as no one knows the Father except the Son and those to whom the Son chooses to reveal him' (Mt 11:25-7). St Teresa does not refer to this scripture passage, to this basic instruction on personal love through which revelation is made, and yet her very first words of comment on the Our Father are certainly in close harmony with it: 'O my Lord, how thou dost reveal thyself as the Father of such a Son, while the Son reveals himself as the Son of such a Father, blessed be thou for ever and ever' (WP, 27). And there is one more point worth noting. When she turns to speak to Christ on this same matter of telling us to call God our Father, she is amazed and delighted that he should 'descend to such a degree of humility as to join with us when we pray' (WP, 27).

Immediately after the passage from St Matthew just quoted, we find Christ saying: 'Come to me, all you who labour and are over-burdened, and I will give you rest. Shoulder my yoke and learn from me for I am gentle and humble in heart' (Mt 11:28). St Teresa goes on talking to God, marvelling at the fact that he is giving us so much by making us his own children and finding no explanation except that he loves so much to give that no obstacle can stop him. One other reflection of hers says he is doing this to make us love to learn what he is teaching us. Finally, she says that rather than write more about it, she will leave it to ourselves to think about. It is a matter deserving repeated attention at length. Here is the very centre of your life, the home from which you go and to which you return. Of its very nature, this relationship with God, your Father, links you to Christ, your Brother, and to all people as your own family. St John had grasped all that very clearly when he was telling us of what we have seen and heard so that we would share it all with himself and be together with him in union with the Father and his Son, Jesus Christ.

Since St Teresa finds in the opening words of the Our Father a real revelation of what God is like, it seems appropriate here to quote the opening of the Vatican II document on Revelation as it too lets us see the loving way in which God makes himself known to us: 'In his goodness and wisdom, God chose to reveal himself and to make known to us the hidden purpose of his will by which through Christ, the Word made flesh, man has access to the Father in the Holy Spirit and comes to share in the divine nature. Through this revelation, therefore, the invisible God out of the abundance of his love speaks to men as friends and lives among them so that he may invite and take them into friendship with himself' (*Dei Verbum,* 2). It yet remains for each of us to come before God and feel out our own relationship and get it right so that it may grow and all we think and do will be firmly rooted in this eternal bond.

The words of the Our Father 'Who art in heaven' bring St Teresa to deal directly with the subject of *Recollection,* the practice of withdrawing our attention from outward things to focus on God within us. So she very logically concludes that we have no need to go to heaven to find him nor to speak in a loud voice to be heard by him but we need only find a place where we can be alone and just look at him who is present within us. He is within me in the house of my heart and can come in humility and confidence and talk to him, ask him for things, tell him my troubles, beg him to set things right for me and yet not fail in my reverance for him. Here St Teresa has something to say about people who will not come close to God on the ground they are not worthy and tells us to avoid this foolish thinking. She does not say so but such an attitude may contain an unwillingness to come close to God because this, of necessity, makes us aware of our sinfulness and calls on us to repent. And St Teresa encourages us to face this by letting us know that he will teach us how to please him. This message is clear, the Lord is within us and we should be there with him. This being within ourselves with him is what she calls the Prayer of Recollection, 'because the soul collects together all the faculties and enters within itself to be with its God' (WP, 28). A special advantage she sees for the soul in this type of prayer is that 'its Divine Master comes more speedily to teach it, and to grant it the Prayer of Quiet, than in any other way' (WP, 28).

St Teresa herself had experienced prayer of a kind that cannot be achieved by our own dedication, or by techniques, but only by a special grace of God. While she tells us time and again that we cannot reach such states of prayer by our own effort she is particularly anxious that we dispose ourselves for this special grace. Indeed, she seems as sure as she can be that we will receive this special grace if we make a habit of recollecting our mind in prayer and persevere in the practice. She says this is like travelling by ship with a favourable wind as compared to walking. You get there so much faster. Genuine recollection can be known by the effects it has on our way of living. It brings out in us a serious effort to do things God's way. All of which is based on the Gospel teaching that where the treasure is there the heart goes. As the heart turns more and more to God within, it ceases to be drawn by things that had attracted it so far. As the habit grows, the eyes are closed in prayer as an outward expression of where the interest is centered. The effort to be recollected has to be a strong persevering one but with practice it becomes much easier, or perhaps it is more correct to say it gets strong as the habit grows. The wish to enter into recollection comes to harvest. This is the world in which the will to sin weakens and the fire of divine love is enkindled because we are alone with him and he is close to us. Some people are confused as to how to imagine God close to us — before us, beside us, within us or just close to us. St Teresa does not see any problem. The place she speaks of as 'within us' is a vast space, a palace of great beauty, incomparably more precious than anything we can see. In it is a special place reserved for our Guest and this is our heart.

Later in life, when her understanding of all this was deeper still, St Teresa returned to the idea and called her finest book, *The Interior Castle*. In that, she spoke first of the soul as a heaven in which God delights. The inner beauty of a life lived for God is, she declares, too beautiful to be described. She goes on to speak of the Mansions of *The Interior Castle* and in so doing describes with great clarity seven stages of prayer. So it is possible to be in this castle with our Lord and still striving to get close to him. The reason is that he does not reveal himself to us in the beginning but has gradually to prepare us for each new understanding of himself that he wants us to have. This is a slow process which we can help along by striving honestly and generously to give ourselves to him more and more in the way we live out each day. The wish to please and serve him and not ourselves is the secret way to deepen our prayer. St Teresa says we should empty the castle so that he can put in and take out whatever he wants. This sounds lovely but it calls for a lot of detachment. And yet, he gives the strength the moment we make the effort. This makes us review our whole set of values until we come more and more to prize the things that last and forget what passses. Values become very much eternal values and much of what we have valued highly seems insignificant. This change of heart and outlook is an immense help to prayer. It opens the way for God to work in us, to make us ready for the gifts he has for us. It is plain to everyone that before God we are very small; if he were to make us suddenly aware of his presence, we would be terrified and he would have to reassure us. It is obvious then that to prepare for his coming we should have a clear idea of just how small we are in his eyes. Indeed, if things happen to make us feel small, we should be glad of them and reflect how close they bring us to the truth. This too prepares us for his gifts. St Teresa says: 'it is best. . . that you should be humbled. . . and wish to be so for the sake of the Lord who dwells in you. Turn your eyes upon yourself and look at yourself inwardly, as I have said. You will find your Master; he will not fail you: indeed the less outward comfort you have, the greater the joy he will give you' (WP, 29).

St Teresa returns to a combination of urgings and instructions to help us acquire the habit of recollection. First, she emphasises the importance of desiring it since it is not something we have to wait for but something we can acquire by our own repeated efforts. She does not expect a lot of us in the beginning: 'If I can recall the companionship I have within my soul for as much as a moment; that is of great utility. . . we should know and abide with the Person with whom we are speaking. . . the whole mischief comes from our not really grasping the fact that he is near us, and imagining he is far away' (WP, 29). It is so very obvious every time she comes back to this that there is work to be done. We must make the effort to get our mind off other things and on to him who is here, near us. It is only with frequent trying that this practice will grow into a habit. It is one more example of the truth of the axiom that where there is a will, there is a way. It is a matter of wanting the greatest thing we can have and of being wise enough to want it badly. One sure result is that we will come, in time, to realise he is aware of what

33

we are saying, listening to us as we pray, and this makes us say the prayers more slowly, and even stop saying them to just be there, aware of him and knowing he is aware of us. This may not last for long but it is the goal we are trying to reach and to arrive even for a little while is a great achievement. From these moments of awareness things we once knew from our own meditations take on a new light as if they had just been taught to us in a new way. He teaches us to be still and know that he is near, that he loves us and he invites us to respond. So, by saying our vocal prayers well, we can grow in this awareness of God within us, loving us, caring for us, God who made us, God who redeemed us, God who changes us until we are like him. This is a simple sure way with little room for error. Do it often and do not give it up. The habit may be acquired in a year but we should be willing to work longer. The very effort has its own rewards.

The emphasis on effort, gentle but persevering is very much a vital part of Teresa's teaching. For those who have experienced the benefit of recollection, the reason for this is clear but for the beginner, it may not be so obvious. St Teresa's purpose, her objective, is union with Christ. He is the one she is seeking and he is so important to us that the desire to reach him, to come close to him should be so strong as to be worthy of him. In the beginning, when the person trying to pray has so little to work on, it is important to be convinced that at the end of this search is the most precious treasure we can possibly find. Prayer is where God reveals himself to us individually and his greatest revelation is his Son, Jesus Christ. He is God's final and clearest Word. All other forms of revelation get fresh light from Christ. We get to know the Father through him; it is his Spirit who is sent to sanctify us. So in the world in which we live, he is the one to attend to. The Father said: 'Hear ye him'. We 'hear' and 'listen' and attend by coming to him in recollection.

The impression of Jesus Christ that we get from St Teresa is one of immense good, a Person who is loving, merciful, generous, humble, patient and yet strong and unafraid. All this may be distant from the beginner, but it becomes clearer as he practises recollection. We may have nothing to say save the words of prayers we have learned, but if we say these slowly they begin to relate to our life and then to his. It may not be easy to focus our attention on him. We may have to try to picture him in ways that will make it easier to keep our minds on him. But, if we are convinced that here is our wealth, our goldmine, we will go on and not give up. So the strong desire of the heart to come to him is vitally important. A habit of prayer is something to strive for through a lifetime. It is God's greatest gift to the soul. Prayer consecrates a man, makes him holy and pleasing unto God, makes him walk the earth with a freer swing, not a slave of the world, but as a free man in Christ.

7. Hallowed be Thy Name — Thy Kingdom Come

This serves as fair introduction to St Teresa's commentary on the petitions of the Our Father, 'Hallowed be Thy Name, Thy Kingdom Come'. Her comments on these give us a fine example of what she means when she tells us to think of what we are saying when we pray. In this case, she reflects on what we are asking for in our petitions. For a start, she even recommends that we ask for light so that we see the implications of what we are petitioning. Then she sees these two petitions as inseparable. Unless God's kingdom comes in us, how can we ever rise to praising his name. She argues from what we hope to be doing in heaven, the perfect kingdom, to what we should be doing now, in this kingdom: 'To me, then, it seems that, of the many joys to be found in the kingdom of heaven, the chief is that we shall have no more to do with the things of earth; for in heaven we shall have an intrinsic tranquillity and glory, a joy in the rejoicings of all, a perpetual peace, and a great interior satisfaction which will come to us when we see that all are hallowing and praising the Lord, and are blessing his name, and that none is offending him. For all love him there and the soul's one concern is loving him, nor can it cease from loving him because it knows him. And this is how we should love him on earth. . .' (WP, 30). This may be regarded as a personal interpretation of a scripture text but it leaves no doubt but that prayer, attention to God, is no academic exercise but a real act of loving God, personal, committed and free from contrary attractions. The experiences of interior prayer are an invitation to the eternal vision of God. What St Teresa is saying can be more readily understood by bearing in mind that the 'Kingdom of God' as we know about it in the Synoptic Gospels can be said to apply to heaven — the perfect kingdom to which we look forward in hope — and to the kingdom among us which we identify with the Church, the new people of God. The kingdom among us, which we also call the Mystical Body of Christ, is found in people. We say Christ is the head of the Church, his Body, because it is his life in us that makes us members of the kingdom here and heirs to the kingdom we seek. Because of this fact that we share in some real way in the life of Christ, he is made present to us to the extent that we can know him by faith and love him with a degree of the same love which comes to perfection in heaven. By recollection, we become aware of his presence in us sometimes by a passing experience that lets us feel his action in us but much more frequently by faith which lets us know he is here even when what we feel does not convey such a message. This presence of God as experienced, mainly by faith alone, is what St Teresa has in mind when she thinks of the kingdom we want to come. This is not a departure from the usual meaning which sees the petition as a prayer that asks for all people to come to believe in Christ because for St Teresa, interior prayer touches the heart of the Church and is very definitely apostolic and contributes in a vast way to the spread of the Gospel.

As God reveals himself to us in prayer, he is making his kingdom come in us and is enabling us to praise his name. When we say these petitions, then, we are not just asking that other people in far away places come to do as we do but that we wake up to what God is doing and make room for him to live in us in a way that we will be more aware of him and he can reveal himself to us more and more. This calls for dedication and unselfish love and, at first, a willingness to be upset by his presence which can make us uncomfortably aware of our own faults.

This growth of awareness of God within us brings St Teresa on to describe a state of prayer in which God intervenes in our efforts to focus on him and gives us an awareness of himself that we cannot bring about by our own efforts. This does not happen suddenly but in a very subtle way so that the first signs of it that we notice are not things that happen in an instant but things that come gradually and amount to a change in our way of praying. If we have developed recollection as a habit of prayer, then we come to a practice, with some variations, whereby we bring ourselves to an awareness of God as someone close, a friend who listens, a good companion even in silence. Then this awareness begins to change until the method that makes us sure he is with us leaves us with a sense of his absence. We try again with the same result. We cannot get the reaction we got before. We cannot pray as we did. This happens even when there is a great desire to communicate with God and no wish to fix our attention on anything else. Not that our thoughts may not wander to other things. They may but even then there is an anxiety because God is somehow 'absent', 'gone away'. This 'absence' goes on and on for a long, long time and is accompanied by a fear that we may have caused it and so gives rise to a great desire to do anything God wants and not to offend him. It is a difficult time and yet a very beneficial time. The only kind of prayer we are capable of now is a kind of attention to God that is very real but impossible to describe as there 'is nothing in it'. It is a kind of blind attention without detail of any kind that we can describe. Yet it gradually brings its own satisfaction. At first it brings the awful fear that we are doing nothing and this is a very testing time but, if it brings the fear of offending God and an agonising wish to 'find' him again, then it is most important we keep it up — just attending to this 'absent' Lord in loving attention that is dark, blind, devoid of feeling or thoughts that tell us anything. We have been given a new and higher way of communicating with God and our first impressions for quite a while are just an awareness of the old ways that have gone out of action. But a new light has come and our silent, anxious, attentive fidelity will turn the winter into spring and the first snowdrop will lead to a garden of flowers. This transition from a way of prayer we had established with long patient practice and some earnest work on doing things God's way to a way we had not known about is a difficult time and one that needs help and direction. But it is good to know of it and to be ready to persevere in it if God grants it to us. St Teresa is so frequently exhorting us to persevere in prayer that it is obvious that the life of prayer by its very nature must call for this resolution to continue at least at certain times. And this is one of those times when continued practice of one way of praying is vital.

Prayer is so definitely a gift of God that it is most helpful and conducive to real knowledge of ourselves to be left helpless at times. If we jump from one way of praying to another, we do not stay long enough in one way to experience long enough our real inability to pray. This experience over a lengthy period develops in us an awareness of our spiritual poverty that will not be forgotten when the Lord grants us higher things and this is vitally important. What we gain from this experience is real humility. In spite of what we think, we get proud of our success in prayer. We give up things, discipline ourselves, and come to some success in that we are able to pray and have a sense of achievement. But when it all changes, we want to switch to something else that will give back that sense of achievement and of being in control of the situation. St Teresa insists that it is by humility that God is led to give us the new way of prayer which we cannot bring about without a special intervention on his part. While we hope and pray that God will grant this to us, while we strive to prepare and dispose ourselves for it, we must not strive to produce it, or to 'practise' it. Our hope must never rest on our worthiness, which would be building on sand but on the loving goodness of God, the rock on which the wise one builds.

So much for the importance of boundless trust and unfathomable humility. We keep our mind on God whom we do not see. The pilgrim's journey is one of faith. Even when certain things reassure us of God's presence, we must not cling to them but always focus on God, whom we do not see as long as we live. When faith and trust and humility have grown as evidence of our sincere generous love, then God lets us know that he is there in the dark. The 'absence' is found to contain the 'presence'. The new awareness comes very delicately at first and more discernibly later. The first stage is often called *Passive Recollection* in the sense that it is a form of recollection in which our attention is somehow 'caught' or controlled by God. In *The Interior Castle,* St Teresa says that when persons are full convinced of the importance of prayer and have been practising recollection, 'the Great King, who dwells in the Mansion within this castle, perceives their good will, and in his great mercy, desires to bring them back to him. So, like a good shepherd, with a call so gentle that they can hardly recognise it, he teaches them to know his voice and not to go away and get lost but to return to their mansion; and so powerful is this shepherd's call that they give up the things outside the castle which had led them astray, and once again enter it' (IC, IV, 3).

This is St Teresa's description of the first awareness of God's special gift of what we call infused or passive prayer. She goes on to comment further. 'Do not suppose that the understanding can attain to him, merely by trying to think of him as within the soul, or the imagination, by picturing him as there. This is a good habit and an excellent kind of meditation, for it is founded on a truth — namely, that God is within us, but it is not the kind of prayer I have in mind' (IC, IV, 3). That is very interesting and comes very naturally from the main truth that we are dealing with something we cannot produce — either by thinking or imagining. Even for those who never come to this stage, it still provides great insights into God and gives a glimpse of how far his ways and thoughts are above ours. We sometimes feel great fervour in our prayer, at least on special occasions; such as, retreats, pilgrimages, greater feasts. This emotion could also be aroused by a national event or the return of a friend or a dramatic performance. The fact that it is directed to God in prayer is a great thing but that does not make it anything more than a lovely human feeling brought about by human means in a religious atmosphere. The Shepherd's call is different in its cause and source. 'It happens only when God is pleased to grant us this favour,' says St Teresa and she gives us some guidelines on how to react. One obvious thing is to praise God for so great a gift. Then we should not strive to reason it out, to master or grasp it with the mind, 'but to be intent upon discovering what the Lord is working in the soul.' She speaks here of attention to and awareness of God. We attend to person and action, not to thought. To get the idea that we should 'go blank' in order let this prayer develop is not correct. 'Let us try, without forcing ourselves or causing any turmoil, to put a stop to all discursive reasoning, yet not to suspend the understanding, nor to cease from all thought, though it is well for us to remember that we are in God's presence and who this God is' (IC, IV, 3). Again, this piece of advice is very valuable to all of us. If at this stage, when God's special action is already evident, we do not try to 'help it on' by blanking out our mind, then it makes no sense to do that at an

39

earlier stage in prayer. There are a number of things we can do to create the right atmosphere for prayer and dispose ourselves for a proper loving attention to God but the whole purpose of all this — giving our attention to a loving God—is ruined if we just go mindless.

Another observation by St Teresa is of interest. At this stage, people experience a great freedom of spirit. Because of the new way of loving God there is less fear of God combined with a strong resolve not to offend him. This resolve finds expression in the careful avoidance of even the danger of offending him. There is a certain confidence of coming into his eternal presence, an anticipation of his welcome that draws us away from whatever is unpleasing to him. And for anyone engaged in meditation such thoughts are valuable, the kind of thoughts that coax us to pray.

Now to return to the Shepherd's call. It is the first signal that the person is coming into a stage or area of prayer that is called the *Prayer of Quiet*. In *The Way of Perfection,* St Teresa is somewhat hesitant to talk about this as she senses that some of those for whom she was writing would not believe that would ever happen to them. She comes to this in the thirtieth chapter where she is commenting on the petitions of the Our Father: 'Hallowed be Thy Name, Thy Kingdom Come'. And she gets into her subject carefully and we might say slyly. She says that unless God's kingdom comes within us, we will not be able to praise his name. So she takes a quick look at what it must be like in heaven so as to get across the point that we must work for and expect some change within us if we are to aspire to that blessed stage. Then she admits the objection that one would need to be an angel to reach that state and answers by telling the story of a person who knew no other way to pray than to say the Our Father and yet, through that, was led by God to pure contemplation. So, the conclusion is obvious; if we are going to say the prayer he taught us with the care it deserves, it is possible that he will teach us things we could never have learned on our own. And so the Prayer of Quiet. All the phrases she uses bring out the fact that it is a gift of God: 'The Lord begins to show us that he is hearing our petition: he begins to give us his kingdom on earth. . . a supernatural state, and, however hard we try, we cannot reach it for ourselves. . . the Lord gives us peace through his presence' (WP, 31). The person praying realises God is very close, feels great reverence, experiences the

40

greatest delight, keeps still. Giving us a closer look, St Teresa says that the functions of the mind are changed. She says that the understanding, imagination and will are stilled, quietened to the point where they are more attentive than they could ever have become by their own effort. The understanding and imagination enjoy a greater realisation of God's presence but they are still free to attend to other objects. The will is captivated, not to the point of losing its freedom, but by giving itself unreservedly to God. 'It is the will that is in captivity now; and, if while in this state it is capable of experiencing any pain, the pain comes when it realises that it will have to resume its liberty' (WP, 31). Persons in this state like to remain motionless, speaking is distressing, they spend a whole hour on a single repetiton of the Our Father. No more is necessary now. God is so close any little sign expresses all their love. Sometimes tears come but without sadness. Joy, delight, praise of God — this is everything. This 'captivity' of the will sometimes shows itself outside prayer time. For a day or two the person in this state can work and attend to business without being fully involved because the strong new bond with the Lord goes on even outside prayer. St Teresa says the person is like Martha and Mary at one time. She follows her description of the Prayer of Quiet with a warning that we cannot bring it about and an anxiety to hold on to it could disturb the peace it brings and so upset it. Yet it does help to use a word or gesture to renew it if it is weakening. She then tries to show that this is not the highest form of prayer. She says this is like a child being fed and having nothing to do but swallow its milk. The *Prayer of Union* is like having the milk placed in the child's stomach with no effort at all on its part.

Again, this kind of prayer, even when we just read about it, tells us a lot. While the will is firmly clinging to God, it is possible for the thoughts and imagination to run wild. So in our ordinary prayers, the will to pray may be quite strong while the mind will not settle and we suffer continuous distractions. What we regard as good prayer or successful prayer is usually the prayer that brings us satisfaction. Such prayer is beneficial but the final test is in the degree to which it pleases God, how it binds our will and heart to him and this is known only to him. Prayer that brings consolation should be pleasing to God, our Father. Prayer that tests and increases our generosity is always a delight to him.

8. Thy Will be Done

What we can learn from St Teresa's descriptions of the *Prayer of Quiet* is that, what the heart and will are about is more important than what is going on in the mind or emotions. And this brings us easily to the next petition of the Our Father: 'Thy will be done on earth as it is in heaven.'

In a way, that is typical of her. St Teresa starts out telling us not to be afraid to offer ourselves to God to let his will be done in us. In her own humorous way, she reminds us that in the end, his will is going to be done if we are to come to any good, so we are not all that generous in telling God to do it his way. 'It amuses me that there should be people who dare not ask the Lord for trials, thinking that his sending them depends on their asking for them' (WP, 32). People may shy away from asking for trials out of humility. They know themselves and realise they are too weak to bear trials. This is very honest as far as it goes, but God gives strength to bear the trials he sends. And the source of this strength comes from our Saviour who, in order to give us this strength, suffered more than he will ever ask of anyone of us. This is the way to eternal life and we save ourselves a lot of anguish and time if we face it firmly and put our hearts into our prayer when we say: 'Thy will be done'. This is not just resignation, it is real willing generous love of God. This is where love sprouts and grows. To do God's will, to stay with his commandments and let the pain involved happen in silence, even to seek ways of giving up things for him, to be ready to suffer in silence as a secret way of loving God — this is the wisdom of the Saints. This is the heart and soul of prayer, of loving God. What our heavenly Father did to his beloved Son is impossible to understand. He sent him to a painful death. No human father would think of such a thing. God's ways are not our ways. And his way of suffering is God's way of loving something in our sin-laden condition which makes it necessary that it should be so. God's mercy is his greatest work but his justice must be satisfied so that our dignity is restored. It is good to recall the case of Abraham who was told to sacrifice his only son. And he set out to do just that. Abraham here was a revelation of God the Father. It was as if God said, 'Can you do what I have to do?' And Abraham's readiness made him worthy of this call. He did not have to make the sacrifice but he had to be ready. He had the wisdom to know that God's will must be done. We can see how St Teresa showed the same insight: 'So you see what God gave his best beloved, and from that you can understand what his will is. These, then, are his gifts in this world. He gives in proportion to the love he bears us. . . He gives in accordance to the courage which he sees that each of us has. . . I believe that love is the measure of our ability to bear crosses, whether great or small' (WP, 32).

So prayer is not just another of the games people play. We cannot make a mockery of God by just promising what we do not mean to perform. Deeds must match words and failures must lead to new effort. This is what makes for sincerity, for honesty, integrity and real love. This petition also leaves us open to all God may send us. When we find his love in adversity — and it is often more difficult to find in small things — it is more refined and more lasting. This, it seems, is the secret wisdom of the saints.

So the gift of our will to God is the real key to very deep prayer. 'What power this gift has! If it be made with due resolution, it cannot fail to draw the Almighty to become one with our lowliness and to transform us into himself and to effect a union between the Creator and the creature. . . the more resolute we are in soul and the more we show him by our actions that the words we use to him are not words of mere politeness, the more and more does our Lord draw us to himself. . . in order to prepare us to receive great favours from him. . . his Majesty never wearies of giving. Not content with having made this soul one with himself, through uniting it to himself, he begins to cherish it, to reveal secrets to it, to rejoice in its understanding of what it has gained and in the knowledge which it has of all he has yet to give it. He causes it gradually to lose its exterior senses so that nothing may occupy it. This we call rapture. He begins to make such a friend of the soul that not only does it restore its will to it but he gives it his own also' (WP, 32).

This is about as far as St Teresa goes in describing the development of Passive Prayer in *The Way of Perfection* but she covers this whole area at length in *The Interior Castle* and those who need such knowledge can study it there. Here she passes on having warned us that we cannot come to these heights by our own effort and that attempting to do so achieves nothing but to spoil the kind of prayer that we are able to make. . . 'You would turn what devotion you had quite cold. You must practise simplicity and humility, for those are the virtues that achieve everything' (WP, 32).

This Prayer of Union is a long way from the simple beginning where we give a little thought to the prayers we say and ask ourselves who it is to whom we are speaking, who we are and what we are saying. Yet it is no more than a God-given deepening in love of that original position. Anyone can see how wise St Teresa is in telling us to begin prayer — and continue it — with a simple awareness that brings us face to face with God. It is so different from trying to act in a way that will impress others or attempting to create any special reactions within ourselves. God alone teaches us to pray and we let him do that by giving him our attention. We are, after all, responding to him, to his love, to his revelation of himself, which is his Son, Jesus Christ.

9. Give Us This Day Our Daily Bread

That commentary on the union of our will with God's is magnificent but perhaps too high for us. And St Teresa realised that too. So, in her commentary on the next petition of the Our Father: 'Give us this day our daily bread', she says that our Saviour knows our weakness and how difficult it is for us to keep our promise to do his Father's will. Keeping this promise is vital and so he must find a way for us to do so in spite of our weakness. The way is simple and yet too great to expect. He will stay with us himself and he will be our strength. He is our daily bread, given to us each day by his Father, by our Father. While this is true of every way in which Jesus is present to us, St Teresa applies it here to the Eucharist in particular. She is amazed at this evidence of God's love for us. The manner of his presence hides all his power and leaves him at our mercy. He can be despised, forgotten, insulted and yet is there and will stay as our food to give us the strength we do not have — to be our strength so that we who could do nothing of ourselves can now change our ways and do the Father's will because of his Son who strengthens us. When we ask God for our 'daily bread' we must not waste our time over passing needs but ask for the highest gift God is offering, his divine Son, that he may live in us and enable us, with him, to do his Father's will. To do all things to please God, not to please ourselves, is real freedom. It allows us to put all our anxieties and worries in God's hands and rely on him to take care of them for us. This may come easily to some but for many, it has to be renewed daily.

When St Teresa gets down to the specific help we get from the Eucharist, she begins with the Blessed Sacrament's healing powers. 'Do you suppose that this most Holy Food is not ample sustenance for the body and a potent medicine for bodily ills? I am sure that it is' (WP, 34). She goes on then to tell about a person she knew who was immediately cured of serious illness and great pain. This is of special interest in our time when the belief in healing through prayers has revived. We have the special case of the anointing of the sick for their cure rather than for a happy death. A part of this sacrament we hope for cures through prayers and trust in God. All such cures come through the power of God, the same power that Jesus used in the Gospel and that Peter invoked to heal the cripple at the entrance to the temple. The fact that we are left a sacrament of healing means that this is a standard part of the Church's ministry. So it is proper for us to expect such effects from the greatest of the sacraments, the Eucharist.

Next to this, St Teresa speaks of faith coming through the Eucharist. Today we are familiar with what we call the Liturgy of the Word at Mass. This is the use of scripture readings and reflection on them to strengthen our faith and so prepare us for the Eucharist. This is the way that Teresa went too because she 'tried to strengthen her faith, when she communicated, by thinking it was exactly as if she saw the Lord entering her house, with her bodily eyes, for she believed in very truth that this Lord was entering her poor abode, and she ceased, as far as she could, to think of outward things, and went into her abode with him' (WP, 34). This brings us right back to recollection, to finding God within us. It is obvious that we can think of God being within us after we have received him in Communion. Not only can we do that at the time but we can recall the memory of it at any time and be helped to become familiar with the fact that God lives in us. St Teresa goes on to say, 'She tried to recollect her senses so that they might all become aware of this great blessing or rather, so that they should

45

not hinder the soul from becoming conscious of it. She imagined herself at his feet and wept with the Magdalen exactly as if she had seen him with her bodily eyes in the Pharisee's house. Even if she felt no devotion, faith told her that it was good for her to be there' (WP, 34).

This makes the Eucharist a sure way to contemplative prayer and the subject brings St Teresa back to some points she made previously, especially one that tells us God is here and not away off in a distant heaven. 'This is something which is happening now; it is absolutely true, and we have no need to go to seek him a long way off. . . He will work miracles when he is within us, if we have faith' (WP, 34). And, of course, the important miracle is to get us the courage to do God's will. But he is so approachable now in this humble disguise that we do not have to lose courage at the sight of repeated failures but can always begin again. Even the two-time loser can have a fresh start. He is here for our benefit and is willing to begin with the very weakest. It is important to bear in mind that Christ is present to us in the Eucharist in a special way. We call it sacramental and a sacrament is a visible sign given power by Christ to produce in us some spiritual effect we could not produce of ourselves. Baptism has a sign of being drowned and rescued or of being dead and coming to life and its effect is to give us a new kind of life for the first time, a sharing in some way in the very life of God. The other sacraments increase this and, if it is lost, Penance restores it. Now the Eucharist is a sacrament under the sign of food—bread and wine—so that its product is a strengthening of existing life. All of which means that, when we receive our Lord himself as a sacrament, he is busy all the time he is present feeding us with new life and giving us the strength to do what was not possible before. Christ is present not just to comfort, console and heal but the *strengthen* us so that we can do his Father's will as he did, make a new beginning and set out with firm resolve to do something good and beautiful, to bring joy to our Father in heaven.

When we receive Jesus Christ, the Son of God, the full payment for all sin, there is no limit to the changes that can take place between us and our Father. We know that lifelong habits will not break easily, that old ways do not change and that miracles are not to be multiplied. It is true that longstanding habits can reduce the scope of our freedom but where there is no freedom, there is no fault and God alone knows us as we are. He can leave us our weaknesses and busy himself with our inner selves, our deeper lives where we are still free and fully capable of doing good and avoiding evil, and can win that inner country for his Father. The world of the sacraments is a whole new world, linked with ours and yet above it. Nowhere do we receive its impact more fully than in the Eucharist.

At Communion time, we are really back to the fountain of life. The answer to all our needs is here. So we call out to God for help and we spell out our needs. But we must bear in mind that he knows a whole lot more about our needs than we do. So there is a lot of wisdom here in just giving our attention to him and let our wonder and love grow in strength of his presence—in the light of his love for us. It is such a still time full of the dawn. 'Remember that this is a very profitable hour for the soul; if you spend it in the company of the good Jesus, you are doing him a great service' (WP, 34). Here is the perfect situation for him to teach you some of the inner meaning of the Our Father. But for that, he needs our attention and as a matter of habit. We must 'stay with him', be with him, recall him, come back to him until he is in reality the centre of our living, the home in which we are fed and loved, from which we go out and to which we return.

10.   Forgive Us Our Trespasses

St Teresa proceeds to another petition by showing the logic of her reasoning up to now. The big thing for us to accomplish is to do God's will. We cannot do this with our own resources alone. So he gives us strength for the task, our daily bread. So, now we can begin, we can come before God ready to do his will but being in his presence makes us again aware of who we are and what our record is and our condition. So we promptly ask to be forgiven our sins. The way in which our Saviour tells us to do that is by teaching us to say 'forgive us our trespasses as we forgive those who trespass against us'. St Teresa is fully aware of the deliberate linking of our forgiveness with the other, of God forgiving our sins and of us forgiving all who offend us. She points out that the petition indicates an existing practice and not just a good resolution. We who crave for forgiveness are forgiving in our own lives. It is God's will that we forgive each other, so that this practice is actually one of the things we are praying for when we say, 'Thy will be done'. So when we forgive, we do his will. So, St Teresa says, 'the saints rejoiced in insults and persecutions: it was because these gave them something to present to the Lord when they prayed to him' (WL, 36). From this idea, she draws some hard conclusions — that she herself has nothing to forgive, that instead of being blamed unfairly, she is not blamed enough because people do not realise how sinful she is. So she says her forgiving is not worth anything and most certainly cannot pay for the forgiveness she is asking of God. By implication, the same goes for you and me.

All this brings her back to the old question of our honour, of standing on our dignity, of nursing a grudge instead of being humble and forgiving in face of our own need for understanding and mercy. If we are to come close to God, then we have to begin to be like him and the place to begin is here: to forgive so that we may be forgiven. We are not losing our reputation — our true honour is to be found in God's salvation of us, not in a passing reputation. St Teresa says it clearly: 'Let my interests be looked after by others — I will forget about myself altogether' (WP, 36). All of this is clearing the ground for a fuller love of each other. If we join our will with God's will, then we want what he wants, not the death of the sinner, but that he be converted and live. We want goodness and joy and peace and unity. God wants us to be like that. He does not want us to be in opposite camps, fighting over rights or possessions. 'How important it is for us to love one another and to be at peace' (WP, 36). This may seem rather idealistic but St Teresa is speaking from the experience of union with God, a form of prayer in which the will is united to God's will without reserve and in the light of this experience she is able to speak with real authority. In fact, she stresses frequently the fact that trials and crosses are good for us at this stage and being slighted by others helps us to grow in this union with God. It brings a great sense of eternal values so that all passing things are noticed less and less. Instead of looking for praise, such people are anxious to be seen for what they are, another example of what the merciful

Lord is doing for a sinner.

Here is a quotation to remember: 'The determination to suffer wrongs, even though such suffering brings distress, is very quickly seen in anyone to whom the Lord has granted this grace of prayer as far as the stage of union' (WP, 36). If this kind of fortitude does not begin to show itself, then any special states of prayer are suspect. So fortitude is a sure sign of the work of the Holy Spirit. He can manifest himself in many ways but if he is making us holy, like to Christ, letting Christ live in us, then a courageous love of the cross will appear. And this is surely a good principle to apply in proper measure at any stage of prayer. The Our Father has its own special insights for people very close to God but it is also the special prayer of all of us. In it each of us can express our individual needs and say what we want to say. We do not have rise above ourselves to pray but simply see ourselves as we are and speak honestly and truthfully to God. When we say the Our Father in this way, we see in the words the meaning that matches our lives and the words we use begin to affect the way we live and this is real prayer. 'If our actions and words are one, the Lord will unfailingly fulfil our petitions. The two things — surrendering our will to God and forgiving others — apply to all. True, some practice them more and some less. . . we will do what we can and the Lord will accept it all' (WP, 37).

11.   Lead Us Not into Temptation

We pray to God, our Father, to lead us not into temptation but to deliver us from evil. Each of us can list some of the temptations and evils we want God to keep away from us, be they persons, places or things and it is good at times to repeat this petition quietly and to mention each of the things we have in mind. This helps to bring our prayer and our day-to-day circumstances together and it makes prayer more real and life more prayerful to do this. From her experience, St Teresa tells us how to apply this petition to our life of prayer. She repeats the very important fact that prayer and the cross work closely together so that it is far more important and infinitely wiser to face up to trials and go that way than to be looking for consolations. When our prayer is fervent it is very important to be humble about it and remind ourselves we are not worthy of this. A great sense of God's generosity and our own unworthiness is what we need when our devotion is strong.

A bigger danger is in thinking we have certain virtues when we don't. This leads to pride and pride goes before a fall, and before we know it we have, as St Teresa says, 'sprained our ankles'. This piece of advice should not be looked upon as a handy rule-of-thumb. This fact is that it is one application of an overall attitude that is absolutely necessary in spiritual matters. We like to grade our progress, to see how we are doing and we do this in order to encourage ourselves. In this frame of mind, we tend to look for signs of progress and to invent or exaggerate them. This is a wrong approach with a very dangerous result. The result is that we put ourselves in an unreal situation, a role for which we are not prepared and we go from one error to another. It is like a person who is not physically fit getting into games. He can very easily sprain an ankle. When we're dealing with spiritual matters, the mistakes of judgment are not all that obvious. This is an icy surface and we have to be alert to keep our balance. The basic mistake here is in comparing ourselves with others or with our own performance at a previous time. This kind of comparison is good if it makes us humble but once it begins to give us satisfaction, then we must go back to the really valuable comparison by which we come face to face with Christ. We begin to pray by placing ourselves before God. In every way we can we should return to this most important basic position.

When the Bible talks of walking before God, aware he is looking at us, it is putting us on the right path. When we turn from God, we are in danger of putting on appearances, acting a role, wearing a mask, but before God we know we have nothing that we have not received and from that beginning we can grow up as people of God. If we watch our day-to-day behaviour, we learn that actually we are very changeable people. The strength we experience on a certain day may be gone the next day; and the assurance which carries us through a whole decade may desert us and leave us without the courage to tackle any situation. St Teresa said this happened to her so regularly that she came to see that whatever virtue she had was just on loan and she is particularly anxious that we

50

take heed of that lesson. God has to keep us humble because this is what we are. If we hold on to this truth, God can give us the virtue we need when we need it. If we make the mistake of thinking the courage or detachment God has given us is something we have acquired and now own, he must leave us without this ability so that we come back to the truth about ourselves. This is the sort of thing we may observe easily enough in another while we fail to see what is happening to ourselves. God gives each new day and we use it all in his service. The next day we ask again for everything we need to serve him and for that alone.

To stay before God and develop a deep permanent sense of how small we are is real wisdom and so we pray God to keep us in the frame of mind and to save us from any temptation to change. St Teresa goes on to point out the difference between thinking we have some virtue and actually being tested in a concrete situation. This too may seem obvious but it can so easily escape the notice of the person to whom it is happening. It is very easy to think we are forgiving people, free from prejudice until we are put to the test. When God sends us trials, it is most important we notice the good they do us and thank him for that. Not so easy but very Christ-like. At certain times in history one virtue or another comes into style and it is fashionable to be seen to practise this. In such an atmosphere, everyone talks a certain language in praise of work, peace, helping the aged or whatever is being promoted at the time. This is good in itself but the individual may be just talking the language and avoid the concrete actions the real situations require. Real solid virtue looks for action not just words or feelings. There are many subtle mistakes whereby we can deceive ourselves and think we are serving God when we are just trying to please ourselves. We need God's guiding hand in this strange world of goal and motives. It is an area through which he must shepherd us, so we pray, Lead us not into temptation. 'The person who is truly humble is always doubtful about his own virtues; very often they seem more genuine and of greater worth when he sees them in his neighbours' (WP, 38).

This living in humility, in honest truth, before God, is a great healer of anxious hearts. It should bring us slowly but surely to realise in actual living that we are completely dependent upon God. We worry about possessions, about friends, about our health

51

and perhaps even more about our reputation. It is a very good thing to talk to God and tell him just what worries us and why. If we keep doing this, we are bound to begin to see that he controls all the things for which we worry. We are anxious because we are not in control. We must learn to be happy that he is in control. This is a hard lesson to learn and yet we cannot afford to live without it. It is a real sign of trust in God's love for us, a sure test of how deeply we believe in that love. 'Stop worrying about yourself and leave God to provide for you, come what may' (WP, 38).

St Teresa has a final word on humility and it is to warn us against a type of it that is not genuine. If people come to know the value of humility and try to deepen it in their lives by coming frequently face-to-face with God, there is something to be avoided in this valuable practice. It is the danger of dwelling on past sins and concluding we are not worthy to be close to God. This could drive people from prayer and even from the Sacraments but, in less severe cases, it can undermine our confidence in God's love for us. There is something in us that keeps telling us God is not interested, is not close, does not care or that all the good things we hear about God's merciful understanding do not apply to us due to some known or hidden fault in us that makes us unworthy. We do not mercifully follow this complex to its logical conclusion where we say our sins are too great to be forgiven but we settle for a middle line which says that we are not good enough to be given any special call from God or to develop a deep friendship with him. Humility certainly makes us aware of our sins but this awareness does not disturb or distress us, rather 'it is accompanied by peace, joy and tranquillity' (WL, 39).

Here St Teresa gives a very valuable piece of advice and all who feel they do not belong close to God should take it to heart and put it into practice regularly: 'When you find yourselves in this state, cease thinking, so far as you can of your own wretchedness, and think of the mercy of God and of his love and his sufferings for us' (WP, 39). This is a very helpful rule for many people whose confidence in God is too weak to be worthy of God. It is a practice that will grow on us until we are lifted out of the mire of fear and we begin to love God.

When we come to this new experience, we should be glad of it and yet not develop another wrong self-image. The same persons who for years made the mistake of thinking they were somehow unclean and just not fit for God's love can now substitute a sense of sinlessness that is again far from the truth. This leads to minimizing real faults and lowering moral standards at least in some matters. This needs to be watched as it can lead to real sinning and can draw the unsuspecting into real sin. It is substituting a new sense of freedom for the reality of being face to face with God. If we can in all honesty tell God that we are doing something to please him and do not believe it is against his will, then all is well. If we have doubts we should consult a confessor or friend who we know will tell us the plain truth. 'However many consolations and pledges of love the Lord may give you, you must never be so sure of yourselves that you will cease to be afraid of falling back again, and you must keep yourselves from occasions of sin' (WP, 39). Our Saviour has taught us to pray to our Father in heaven asking him to steer us clear of temptation and in her reflections on that St Teresa gives us some of the mistakes people make when trying to practise prayer. In so doing, she becomes aware that such warnings could lead people to conclude that it might be safer not to do too much praying. So she hastens to correct such thinking. She says that people who say the Our Father sincerely will not go astray: 'This road is a safe one and you will the more readily escape from temptation if you are near the Lord than if your are far away from him' (WP, 39). And that surely makes a whole lot of sense.

12. Love and Fear

She summarises a good deal of her advice by saying that 'the best way. . . is to use the love and fear given us by his Majesty. For love will make us quicken our steps, while fear will make us look where we are setting our feet. . .' (WP, 40). When St Teresa or any saint, speaks of the fear of God, they are not talking of a scrupulous fear nor of fear such as one experiences under the rule of a tyrant. No, it is a fear of offending God that is actually an expression of our love of God and a sure sign that we genuinely love him. Knowing our own ability to sin, we are afraid not just because of the wrath of God that it might bring but because we genuinely love God and, as a practical development of that, do not want to offend the greatest Friend we have. Of our nature we are afraid and the correct way to handle fear is to focus it on what is really to be feared. If I am afraid of God because I know he can punish me for sin, that is a healthy fear and, when higher motives do not appeal to me, it will keep me from offending him.

The desire to please God contained in this kind of fear is practical and somewhat self-centered but it is still to be highly respected and was taught by Jesus himself. That is just applying good common sense to the eternal implications of our actions. The motivation is not perfect but, none the less, rich and to be commended. As this healthy fear of God becomes refined, it is concerned with not offending God because of his goodness. When Jesus said: 'I do always the things that please my Father', he gave us a perfect standard to follow. He did not say: 'I try to do what pleases my Father.' No, he always did it and there was no failure. He was human like us except in one area. He was without sin. We work from a basis of being redeemed sinners. So we come to the work of pleasing our loving Father with the knowledge that we have within us the ability and even the inclination to offend him and a history and habit of offending him. So our fear of offending him is rooted in an honest knowledge of ourselves. St Paul reminded himself that he once persecuted the church. St Augustine knew that he could easily slip back into his former sinful ways. This is honest thinking and we do well to imitate it. Do not take the risk of driving God away by serious sin. Do not restrain his love by any kind of deliberate sin. In our relationship love and fear work close together. St Teresa gives us some signs whereby we can discern the way they work. She is quite eloquent when she speaks of the love of God and admits she rambles on because she likes to talk about it: 'Those who really love God love all good, seek all good, help forward all good, praise all good, and invariably join forces with good men and help and defend them' (WP, 40). This love cannot be hidden. It will show its language, action and a consistent way of life. When it is not so strong then, frequent prayer, a sense of our own littleness and a sincere pleading with God to save us from offending him are genuine signs of the beginning of his love in us and gives cause for us to hope for a greater degree of that love.

No matter how many years have gone by it is never too late to put ourselves on the way of God's great gift of love. St Teresa has something special to say about this: 'May his Majesty be pleased to grant us to experience this before he takes us from this life, for it will be a great thing at the hour of death, when we are going we know not whither, to realise that we shall be judged by One whom we have loved above all things. . . we shall not be going into a foreign land, but into our own country, for it belongs to him whom we have loved so truly and who himself loves us' (WP, 40). The picture of God that comes through to us in that passage is very revealing. He is the One who loves us and gives us his home to be ours forever. Clearly his love is to be sought diligently at all times. Those who seek this supreme gift and know their own weakness will try to steer clear of everything that leads them to offend goodness. This care not to offend is so strongly advocated by St Teresa that she says we should be willing to die a thousand times rather than deliberately offend God in a serious way, and that it should be unthinkable for us even in a small matter. Yet she makes it clear that people who get so strict as to be inhuman just turn people away from prayer and she never intended that. 'Be as pleasant as you can without offending God. . . get on as well as you can with those you have to deal with, so that they may like talking to you and want to follow your way of life and conversation, and not be frightened and put off by virtue' (WP, 41).

13.   Deliver Us from Evil

The final chapter in *The Way of Perfection* is on the concluding words of the Our Father, 'Deliver us from evil. Amen.' St Teresa's reflection on this is very much that of a saint. To her it was a prayer to be delivered from the misery of this life and brought immediately into the everlasting joys of heaven. She says Jesus prayed for this because his life was so full of suffering. She asks for it because she is only a sinner and getting worse instead of better. It is foolish to want to live on and on: 'I shall find no redress in this life, so I ask the Lord to deliver me from all evil "for ever". What good thing shall we find in this life, in which we are deprived of our great Good and are absent from him? Deliver me, Lord, from this shadow of death, deliver me from all these trials, deliver me from all these pains; deliver me from all these changes, from all the formalities with which we are forced to comply for as long as we live, from all the many, many, many things which weary and depress me' (WP, 42). This eloquent outburst may be beyond your own reactions but it is worth your while to reflect that you must pass on from here and that no one has seen, heard or even imagined the good things waiting for you. This exercise of 'joyful hope' is a great way to become detached from all the things we cling to with a mere fingerhold. Also, when we ask to be delivered from evil, we are not asking to be free of all pain and endure nothing in God's service. We ask to be free of offending God and then to serve him in a state of sacrifice and joy. But we are asking that in the end heaven will be ours and we will be saved from all evil. It is the big request that we should make with confidence. We are talking to God who can give us anything and wants with all his heart to give us everything: 'What does it cost me to ask it, since we ask it of One who is so powerful? It would be insulting a great emperor to ask for a farthing' (WP, 42).

Here this unique commentary on the Our Father stops. But she still has a few things to emphasise: 'You see now, friends, what is meant by perfection in vocal prayer, in which we consider and know to whom the prayer is being made, who is making it and what is its object. When you are told it is not good for you to practise any but vocal prayer, do not be discouraged, but read this with great care and beg God to explain to you anything about prayer which you cannot understand. For no one can deprive you of vocal prayer or make you say the *Pater Noster* hurriedly, without understanding it. If anyone tries to do so, or advises you to give up your prayer, take no notice of him' (WP, 42). In that short passage we can hear a whole lot of echoes of things said before: the value of praying frequently in honest simplicity alone with God who loves us. She is amazed at all that is contained in the Our Father, so much that we do not really need any other method of praying and can even get on without any other instruction apart from what is to be got from this prayer: 'Our books may be taken from us, but this is a book which no one can take away, and it comes from the lips of the Truth himself, who cannot err' (WP, 42).

And so we have come to see that prayer is not the achievement of the highly skilled nor of those trained in techniques. It is the gift of God given to anyone who believes in his love and speaks to him humbly, sincerely, frequently and with the faithful perseverance that love requires. It is possible for you and me. The question is not have I been called but, am I resolved to answer the call? The answer comes today, not tomorrow. Today means yes, tomorrow means no. The concluding words of *The Way of Perfection* remind us that it is a very good thing to praise God frequently. She says: 'Blessed and praised be the Lord, from whom comes all the good that we speak and think and do. Amen' (WP, 42).

Notes